YOUR LAND
AND
MY LAND
AFRICA

We Visit

MADAGASCAR

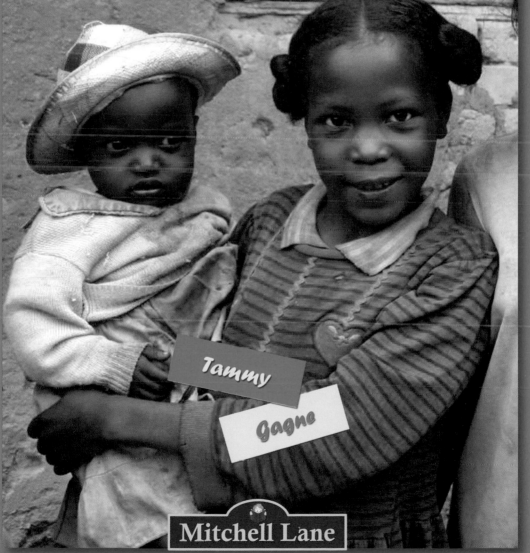

Tammy

Gagne

Mitchell Lane

PUBLISHERS
P.O. Box 196
Hockessin, Delaware 19707

YOUR LAND AND MY LAND AFRICA

Egypt
Ethiopia
Ghana
Kenya
Libya
Madagascar
Morocco
Nigeria
Rwanda
South Africa

YOUR LAND
AND
MY LAND
AFRICA

We Visit

MADAGASCAR

LIBYA

EGYPT

Aswān

SUDAN

Addis Ababa

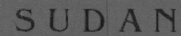

tasco

Mitchell Lane

PUBLISHERS

Printing   1   2   3   4   5   6   7   8   9

Library of Congress Cataloging-in-Publication Data
Gagne, Tammy.
 We visit Madagascar / by Tammy Gagne.
      p. cm. — (Your land and my land. Africa)
 Includes bibliographical references and index.
 ISBN 978-1-61228-305-0 (library bound)
1. Madagascar—Juvenile literature. I. Title. II. Series: Your land and my land (Mitchell Lane Publishers). Africa.
 DT469.M26G18 2012
 969.1—dc23
                                                             2012009624
eBook ISBN: 9781612283791

PUBLISHER'S NOTE: This story is based on the author's extensive research, which she believes to be accurate. Documentation of this research is on page 61.

    The internet sites referenced herein were active as of the publication date. Due to the fleeting nature of some websites, we cannot guarantee they will all be active when you are reading this book.

                                                             PLB

Contents

Introduction.. 6

1　Much More Than a Movie 9

　Where in the World Is Madagascar?... 11

　Facts at a Glance 13

2　So Close, Yet So Far 15

3　A Short History, A Long Struggle 27

4　No Man is an Island 31

5　Playing Its Part in the World 39

6　A Different Kind of Vacation 43

7　Culture and Lifestyle 47

8　Celebrations in Madagascar............... 53

Madagascar Recipe: Banana Fritters....... 56

Madagascar Craft: Raffia Placemats 57

Timeline 58

Chapter Notes.. 59

Further Reading 60

　Books 60

　On the Internet 60

　Works Consulted 61

Glossary... 62

Index 63

Introduction

Africa is the origin of the human species. The oldest known fossils of *Homo sapiens* have been unearthed in Ethiopia, a country that lies just north of the equator. Consisting of fifty-seven countries in all, Africa is the second-largest continent in the world, and the second-most populous one, as well. From Egypt and Libya in the north to Botswana and Zimbabwe in the south, no other area of the world is more filled with history.

Today Africa continues to be the setting for historical events of all kinds. In 2011, the nation of South Sudan gained its independence from Sudan. Unfortunately, not all of what is happening on the continent is to be celebrated. Poverty and war are widespread—and unlikely to end anytime soon. These problems often seem as big as the continent itself.

The island of Madagascar, located to the east of Africa's coast, is at once large and small. Compared to the entire continent of Africa, Madagascar seems downright tiny. To the people who live on this island

Sunset on Lavanono
beach, Madagascar

AFRICA

MADAGASCAR

nation, it also seems much more remote than it really is. Only a couple hundred miles separate Madagascar from the mainland, but everything about the island is different from the countries of its massive neighbor. Most of the animals and plants that live on this island cannot be found anywhere else in the world. The people of Madagascar possess strong ties to both the island and one another. Very few venture beyond the natural borders created by the Indian Ocean and the Mozambique Channel. It seems as though the rest of the world is moving into the future at record speed, but Madagascar is taking its own time getting there.

While life on Madagascar might make the island feel small to its inhabitants, its expansive geography is undeniable. The scenic terrain includes miles upon miles of coastline, inland mountains, tropical rainforests, and deserts. Each region offers its own climate, vegetation, and way of life. To some, the various areas may even seem like different worlds unto themselves.

The red lemur is just one of many lemur species that inhabit the island of Madagascar.

Much More Than a Movie

Just east of mainland Africa in the Indian Ocean lies one of the most unique islands in the world. It is called Madagascar. About 165 million years ago, Madagascar was part of continental Africa. The island broke apart from the mainland as a result of continental drift. At one time, all the continents of the world formed a single land mass that we now refer to as Pangaea (Greek for "all land"). Over time, this large area of land broke into pieces due to weaknesses in the earth's crust.

Madagascar now sits 250 miles (400 kilometers) off the African continent with the Mozambique Channel between them. If you look at the eastern and western coasts of Madagascar, you will notice one major difference. The eastern side is remarkably straight and smooth, whereas the western side has numerous bays and inlets. You can almost see how the island once fit against the mainland.

When many people hear the word Madagascar, they think of the movies with the same name. You may be picturing all the zany creatures and the lush jungle setting of the films right now. Madagascar is indeed home to some of the most diverse animal and plant life on the planet. About 85 percent of these species can only be found on the island.[1]

The best-known animal from Madagascar is the lemur. You may have seen this monkey-like creature on the PBS television show called *Zoboomafoo*. Ninety percent of the world's lemur species are found on Madagascar. Many other unusual wildlife species also inhabit the island. Some look like odd mixes of animals from other parts of the

The rare Tomato frog

world. Others have never been seen by most humans, because they live so deep in the rainforests.

Two of the reasons for Madagascar's wide variety of animals and plants are the island's varied climate and its terrain. From the jungle to the desert, each region offers the ideal environment its own specific fauna and flora need. Not everything about this beautiful island is ideal, though.

Madagascar suffers from some severe conservation problems. A large amount of the land that nurtures so many animal and plant species has been taken over by people. This habitat loss has caused numerous species to become threatened or endangered. Sadly, some have become extinct already. An increasing human population has taken the situation from bad to worse.

Early settlers on Madagascar prepared the soil for planting their rice using a method they called *tavy*. People in the Western Hemisphere often refer to tavy as the slash-and-burn method. When sections of forests are cut and the land is burned, the topsoil becomes very rich. But time is required for the forest to grow back, so the process can be repeated. When land became limited in Madagascar, farmers stopped giving the earth the resting time it needed. They were faced with the choice of planting too soon or not being able to feed their families. For a while this worked well enough, but eventually many of the forests were permanently destroyed.

The plants that are native to the rainforest grow so well there because the conditions are just right for them. Each plant is also part of

WHERE IN THE WORLD IS MADAGASCAR?

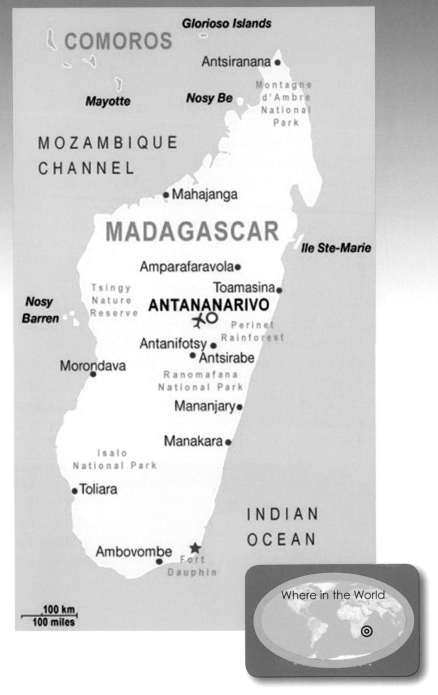

a more complex system that helps every other living thing thrive. The plants even help keep the soil rich with nutrients. When the trees are removed, though, the intense sunlight kills the plants and burns the soil. With no plants left to keep the topsoil in place, it simply washes away with the rain.

Madagascar is sometimes called the Great Red Island because of the deep red color of its topsoil. As it washes to lower ground, this topsoil runs into the ocean. Astronauts have seen the color from space. They say it looks like the island is bleeding.[2]

The people of Madagascar are trying to preserve the areas of their island that haven't been ruined by merciless farming. Environmentalists are also working to help the island bring some of its destroyed areas back to life. Four different nature reserves on the island are now dedicated to scientific research for this purpose. In addition to these efforts, twenty national parks and numerous land reserves have been created.

Farming must continue, of course. Without it, the people of the island can't survive. They must learn new ways of growing food, however. Tavy has been part of the island's culture for so long, the people don't know how to grow crops without it. They also know that they can't keep destroying their forests. The Malagasy have a saying —*tsy misy ala, tsy misy rano, tsy misy vary,* which means, "if there is no more forest, there will be no more water; if there is no more water, there will be no more rice."[3]

Malagasy farmers need to feed their families, but the land also requires time to recover between farming cycles.

MADAGASCAR FACTS AT A GLANCE

Malagasy flag

Full name: Republic of Madagascar

Official languages: Malagasy, French, English

Population: 22,005,222 (July 2012 estimate)

Land area: 224,534 square miles (581,540 square kilometers); roughly twice the size of Arizona

Capital: Antananarivo

Government: Republic

Ethnic makeup: Eighteen Malagasy tribes; small groups of Comorans, French, Indians, Creoles, Chinese.

Religions: Traditional native beliefs 52%, Christian 41%, Muslim 7%

Exports: vanilla, coffee, cotton, cloves, shellfish, apparel, gemstones

Imports: food, petroleum, capital goods, vehicles, consumer goods

Crops: rice, coffee, vanilla, sugar, cloves, cotton, sisal, peanuts, and tobacco

Average high temperatures:

    Toamasina: January 86°F (30°C), August 76°F (24°C)

    Ambovombe: January 88°F (31°C), July 76°F (24°C)

    Antananarivo: January 78°F (26°C), July 67°F (19°C)

Average annual rainfall:

    Toamasina: 128 inches (325 centimeters)

    Ambovombe: 59 inches (150 centimeters)

    Antananarivo: 54 inches (137 centimeters)

Highest point: Maromokotro—9,436 feet (2,876 meters)

Longest river: Betsiboka—326 miles (525 kilometers)

Description of flag: Madagascar's flag has three colors, arranged in three rectangles. The entire left side of the flag is a vertical rectangle of white, which represents purity. To the right there is a horizontal red rectangle on top for sovereignty and a green one just below it for hope.

National sport: Although Madagascar has no official national sport, the Malagasy enjoy many athletic activities including boxing, football (soccer), judo, track and field events, basketball, and tennis.

National flower: Poinciana *(Delonix regia)*

National tree: Baobab tree

Source: *CIA World Factbook:* Madagascar

Nosy Komba is a tiny island that lies off the northwest coast of Madagascar, between Nosy Be and the mainland. This island is home to a type of black lemur called maki macaco.

So Close, Yet So Far

Because Madagascar is so close to Africa, many people assume that the island's environment is similar to that of the mainland. Technically, this is true. You will find mountains, plateaus, tropical jungles, grassy plains, and deserts on both the African continent and the island of Madagascar. The difference is that these diverse types of terrain are spread throughout Africa's 11 million square miles (30 million square kilometers). Every single one can also be found within Madagascar's 224,534 square miles (581,540 square kilometers).

Madagascar is far from small, however. It is the fourth-largest island in the world, not counting the "island continent" of Australia. It measures 976 miles (1,571 kilometers) long and 360 miles (579 kilometers) wide at its widest point. The only islands that are larger are Greenland, New Guinea, and Borneo. Madagascar is just a little smaller than the state of Texas—or about as big as Illinois, Indiana, Iowa, Pennsylvania, and Ohio combined.

Madagascar's mainland is surrounded by several smaller islands. Nosy Be (the word *nosy* means "island") is off the northwest coast. Nosy Boraha (also known as Saint-Marie) is off the northeast coast. Malagasy live on both these islands. Nosy Mitsio, the Radama Islands, Chesterfield Island, and the Barren Islands are a bit farther away in the Mozambique Channel. They are all too small to support permanent inhabitants.

Rice is one of the most popular crops grown in Madagascar. Rice fields are often found alongside houses, like this one in Antananarivo.

An 800-mile (1,287-kilometer) long plateau called the Central High Plateau runs northeast to southwest near the middle of the island. The capital of Madagascar, Antananarivo, is located on this plateau. The plateau is bordered by the Great Cliff, which is a sharp drop as high as 2,000 feet (600 meters) in some places. A smaller, lower cliff called the Betsimisaraka Escarpment sits just to the east of the Great Cliff. A mountain range called the Tsaratanana Massif stands to the north of the plateau. The tallest peak, Maromokotro, measures 9,436 feet (2,876 meters). This is the highest point of the entire island. Two smaller mountain ranges lie to the south. One is Ankaratra, a large cluster of dormant volcanoes near the center of the island. Interestingly, small lakes have formed in some of the craters here. The tips of other ancient volcanoes make up tiny islands off the northwest coast of Madagascar. The other smaller mountain range is the Andringitra in the south. The land running from both the east and west coasts inward is essentially divided by these high-elevation landforms.

The eastern and western sections of Madagascar couldn't be more different from each other. They aren't even similar in size. The land that makes up the eastern coast of the island is narrow—only about 30 miles (48 kilometers) wide. This region consists of marshy plains with fertile soil. The climate is wet and windy with significant rainfall. Maroantsetra, on Antongil Bay, receives the most rain: 138 inches (350 centimeters) a year. The reason for Maroantsetra's rainy weather is its trade winds. These intense air currents bring heavy rain to the east coast all year long. All this precipitation makes the foliage here the greenest on the island.

The eastern coastline runs remarkably straight for most of its 1,000 miles from southwest to northeast. The shores consist of white sand beaches and stunning coral reefs. As inviting as this side of Madagascar may seem, the waters can be treacherous. In addition to its rough waves, the warm Indian Ocean also brings sharks to the area. The rivers on this side of the island include the Mananara, the Mangoro, and the Maningory. Because they are so short and steep, even these fresh waterways include rough areas. Raging rapids and magnificent waterfalls make for spectacular views, but dangerous travel.

Another part of what makes the eastern coast dangerous is its cyclone season. Cyclones are storms with severe winds similar to the hurricanes that hit the east coast of the United States during the summer months. Both types of storms bring heavy rain, high winds, and flooding. Cyclones that have hit Madagascar in the past have killed hundreds of people, destroyed rice fields, and ravaged the forest. Even after the storms have passed, they often leave the survivors exposed to diseases like cholera when flood waters spread bacteria.[1] Cyclones form in the Indian Ocean and strike Madagascar's eastern coast between December and March. Because this island is in the Southern Hemisphere, its seasons run opposite to ours. Summer in Madagascar occurs between November and April.

Although temperatures vary somewhat from one region to another, it's always relatively warm on Madagascar. December is the hottest month of the year. Temperatures at this time are typically between 61°F (16°C) and 84°F (29°C). July is Madagascar's coolest month, with temperatures averaging 50°F (10°C) to 78°F (26°C).[2] The coolest spots are inland at the higher elevations. Nighttime temperatures in the mountains sometimes even drop below freezing.

The western side of the island is between 60 and 125 miles (97 and 201 kilometers) wide, depending on the exact location. Wide, flat plains and low hills make up the landscape. The beaches here are just as breathtaking as the ones on the eastern coast, but the water is much calmer. The climate is also dryer. Unlike the straight eastern coastline, the western coast is made up of numerous tiny bays, coves, and coral reefs. Several rivers run through the western side of the island. These include the Betsiboka, the Onilahy, the Mangoky, the Sofia, and the Tsiribihina. These waterways are longer, wider, and slower than the rivers to the east.

One thing that both coasts do have in common is the presence of coral reefs. These colorful ridges of rocky material are actually living sea creatures called polyps. Coral reefs act as barriers that protect

The coral reefs of Madagascar

Like people, lemurs have opposable thumbs on their hands, but did you know that they also have thumbs on their feet? Having four thumbs helps them climb and swing from branches much better than most other animal species.

Madagascar's beaches from the harsh ocean waves. They also provide a safe haven for many small fish species. Sadly, some of Madagascar's beaches are now at risk of washing away, because the coral reefs have been destroyed. Many of the Malagasy people are very poor. In some areas, indoor plumbing and sewers are not available. Human waste is dumped on the beaches to be washed away in the ocean. Large amounts of waste destroy the coral reefs. If something isn't done about this problem, these beautiful beaches could be lost.

As dry as Madagascar's western coast is, it is not nearly as dry as the land in the southern region of the island. This is where the desert regions are located. Toliara receives just 14 inches (36 centimeters) of rain each year.[3] Three separate rivers run through the south of Madagascar: the Mandrare, the Menarandra, and the Linta. All recede during the dry season. They often run completely dry in between annual rainfalls.

More than 10,000 different plant species live on Madagascar.[4] Most of these live in the rainforests. Many are in danger of becoming extinct; others are already gone forever. Scientists are trying to save as many species as they can, but because there are so many, some have died out even before they could be named. The biggest threats to the island's endangered vegetation are farming, the timber industry, and the Malagasy's steady use of charcoal. Eighty percent of the country's fuel needs are served by wood and charcoal, a byproduct of burning trees. When the trees are cut down, the plants that need their shade have little to no hope of surviving.

One of the most magnificent plants that lives on Madagascar is the orchid. More than 1,000 different species of this delicate flower grow on the island.[5] Orchids can be found in every part of the country. At higher elevations they grow on the ground at the base of trees. On the

The star-shaped petals of Madagascar's Angrae-cum Orchid have inspired several nicknames. The flower is also known as the Comet Orchid, the Christmas Orchid, and the Star of Bethlehem Orchid.

east coast, they grow on tree branches. Surprisingly, these orchids don't even need soil.

One of the best-known trees on Madagascar is the ravinala palm tree. The fronds (or branches) of this unusual species of palm look a lot like the branches on the palm trees you may have seen in Florida. The difference is in how the ravinala fronds are arranged on the tree. They spread out to make the tree look like a giant fan. The base of the leaf stalk is filled with water like a cactus. The Malagasy value this tree greatly, and they have made it one of their national symbols.

If the ravinala is the best-known tree on Madagascar, the baobab tree is the most unusual looking. This tree looks as though it grew out of the ground upside down. Branches that look more like roots grow out of the top. The trunks of the baobab trees are wide and textured with no outshoots at all. They look as if they have been covered with burlap bags. The trunks can hold substantial amounts of water—as much as 32,000 gallons (120,000 liters). For this reason, the baobab is also called the bottle tree.

Baobab trees are extremely hardy. They can live for several thousand years. Unlike most trees, this species can even survive having its bark stripped away. The Malagasy use the bark to make cloth, baskets, and even medicine. They also eat the tree's leaves and drink the pulp of its fruit. They call this tree *reniala,* which means "mother of the forest." Of the eight baobab species in the world, six are found only in Madagascar. The others grow in Africa and Australia.

Exotic animals live on both Madagascar and in countries on the mainland of Africa. But Madagascar is unique because of the types of animals found there. The lemurs alone make up a group of more than thirty species that are found no other place on earth. Many people mistakenly think that lemurs are monkeys. They are indeed related to monkeys, but lemurs are actually the closest living descendents of the monkeys' ancestors—kind of like long-lost cousins one hundred times removed.

Lemurs hunt for food at night and sleep during the day. Their resting holes inside of trees are located only short distances from the places where they forage for food in the forest.

Lemurs range in size. For example, the pygmy mouse lemur is only about 8 inches (20 centimeters) long, including its tail. Its head and body are only 2.5 inches (6 centimeters) long. The entire animal can weigh as little as 1 to 2 ounces (28 to 57 grams). This tiny lemur is the smallest primate in the world. On the other end of the scale, there are the indri lemur and the diademed sifaka lemurs. Both of these species are comparable in size to a large cat. The indri lemur weighs between 15 and 22 pounds (7 and 10 kilograms), while diademed sifaka lemurs average 13 pounds (6 kilograms).

The best-known species is the ring-tailed lemur, which typically weighs a little less than 5 pounds (2.3 kilograms). This species is named for the black and white stripes that "ring" its tail. Most people know this species because it lives mainly on the ground. Tourists who visit

The ring-tailed lemur is the easiest for most people to recognize. As its name implies, it has a long striped tail that looks like a black and white stack of rings.

The fruit bat is just one of the many animals at Madagascar's Berenty Reserve.

Madagascar's Berenty Reserve are often greeted by these lemurs. They are extremely social with both each other and people. You may have seen this type of lemur in a zoo or on television.

About half the species of lemurs are nocturnal. The aye-aye is among the species that are more active at night. Many people think this species is the oddest. It is said to look like a squirrel with an owl's eyes, a bat's ears, and a fox's tail. Travel writer Hilary Bradt has said, "The aye-aye seems to have been assembled from the leftover parts of a variety of animals."[6] The aye-aye has a bony middle finger that it uses for digging food out of the ground. The Malagasy people believe the aye-aye brings bad luck. There is a superstition that this lemur uses its middle finger to point out the next person who will die. For this reason, many members of this species have been killed.

The Malagasy feel very differently about the indri lemur. They call this beloved species *babakoto,* which means "little father." Cultural tradition forbids the killing of this species.

Each lemur species has its own diet, habitat, and way of life. The various species live in different regions of the island. Some are ground dwellers, like the ring-tailed lemur. Others spend most of their lives swinging from tall trees, like the indri. Each species survives on a unique combination of vegetation and insects. This makes conservation very important. If the lemurs' habitats aren't protected, the world could lose entire species of this charming animal.

Madagascar is also home to another fascinating animal: the chameleon. Between one-half and two-thirds of all the chameleon species

The fossa is a cat-like animal. It looks a lot like a small cougar.

in the world are found on Madagascar. These tiny reptiles can actually change the color of their skin, appearing to be green, gray, blue, red or brown—all depending on the circumstances. Each animal's color range is a bit different.

Chameleons cannot change to any color of the rainbow, however. Their appearance depends on the light, temperature, and even their mood. They change colors to attract mates or to look more threatening —not to blend in with their surroundings.

Most people don't know that chameleons have another exceptional ability. They can move their eyes in two different directions at the same time. Because each eye has a visual range of 180 degrees, these creatures can see virtually everything around them without ever moving their heads.

Madagascar's largest predator is the fossa, an unusual species that is only found on this island. It is related to the mongoose, but it looks and acts a lot more like a cougar. It actually shares many traits with other big cats, from long whiskers to retractable claws. The fossa hunts birds and small mammals like lemurs. Fossas live throughout the forests of the island.

Most of the animal species found on Madagascar are small. Compared to the great beasts of the African mainland, Madagascar's wildlife can seem downright tiny. When larger animals like giraffes, elephants, and rhinos were developing, Madagascar was already hundreds of miles away. Smaller species likely migrated to the island from the mainland by flying across or floating on logs and other foliage in the Mozambique Channel. These animals then evolved into the ones that exist today.

Many of the animals that made the journey are now gone. Fifteen or more lemur species have become extinct over the last 2,000 years. One was the size of a gorilla. Another species that didn't survive was the elephant bird. This animal is one of the largest birds that ever lived. Believed to be a relative of the ostrich, it stood 10 feet (3 meters) tall. Archaeologists still find their enormous eggs on the southern part of the island.

The unusual-looking baobab tree is Madagascar's official national tree. These trees have been growing on the island for thousands of years.

Chapter 3

A Short History, A Long Struggle

Compared to other areas of the world, Madagascar has a relatively short history. No evidence of ancient human life has ever been found on the island. Archaeologists have never unearthed bones or fossils from ancient people. Historians tell us that the island broke away from the mainland before human life began to develop in other areas of the world.

The first settlers to Madagascar arrived on the island more than 2,000 years ago.[1] They are called the Vazimba. Stories about these Malagasy ancestors have been passed down through the generations on the island. Today the Malagasy think of the Vazimba as the island's guardians.

One might assume that these people came from Africa, since the continent is so close, but this is not the case. It is believed that they actually traveled to Madagascar from the island Indonesia. No one is sure whether these earliest inhabitants sailed directly to Madagascar over 4,000 miles (6,440 kilometers) of ocean or if they traveled closer to the coastlines of India, the Middle East, and Africa. If the latter theory is true, the migration probably took much longer. They probably met and married new people along the way. This would mean that today's Malagasy share a lineage with both the Indonesians and the inhabitants of these other areas.

Beginning around the 7th century, more people migrated to Madagascar, including Muslim traders from the Middle East. At this time, the Sumatrans controlled trade in the Indian Ocean. Remains of forts built by Arab traders during the 9th century can be found on the island. These traders also left their mark on the Malagasy culture by way of their language. Many Malagasy words, including the ones they use for the days of the week, have roots in Arabic.[2]

It took the Europeans a bit longer to reach Madagascar. The first explorers from this part of the world reached the island at the beginning of the 16th century. Portuguese sailors of this era were known for their excellent navigational skills. However, historians believe that they came across the island of Madagascar by accident. The discovery might have been the result of a storm that the Portuguese explorer Diego Dias's fleet encountered in 1500.

The Malagasy people did not use the name Madagascar at this time, and the names they did use were not consistent throughout the island. Some referred to their island as *izao tontolo izao,* which means "the whole world." Others called it *ny anivon'ny riaka,* meaning "in the midst of the waters." In the 13th century, Marco Polo was the first to call the island Madagascar, but only because he mistook it for the Somali capital Mogadishu. When Diego Dias arrived, he called it São

Madagascar got its name from Marco Polo, the 13th century Italian explorer. It was a bit of a mix-up, however. When he heard tales of the Somali capital of Mogadishu, he thought the travelers were actually referring to the island now known as Madagascar.

Lourenço, unaware that it had already been named previously. Madagascar, however, became the preferred name for the island.[3]

The Portuguese tried to settle on the island and convert its inhabitants to Catholicism. Their efforts were met with angry resistance, however. The Malagasy adamantly refused to adopt this foreign religion, and the Portuguese eventually abandoned their plans.

British sailors made their way to Madagascar during the middle of the 17th century. Ships of the British East India Company stopped at the island during their journeys farther east. Other British sailors sought out Madagascar after hearing stories of great riches that existed there. They eventually realized that these stories were just that—stories. The island was not full of gold, silver, and gemstones as a book from this time period suggested. Still, many learned this lesson the hard way. One ship of British sailors tried to colonize the island. It is said that while the Brits were building a fort, the native people asked for their help in a battle. They might have fared better if they had agreed. Instead, they refused, and most of them were killed.

In 1648, Étienne de Flacourt of the French East India Company took over control of a new settlement on Madagascar. He and his group fared slightly better than the Portuguese or British. Still, they faced many challenges. These included exposure to new diseases and persistent battles with the native people. Eventually, Flacourt's group also left the island. He was credited with some important accomplishments, though. He wrote the first descriptions of the island and even created the first written record of the Malagasy language.

This wouldn't be the last of the French involvement in Madagascar, however. Most of the French settlers left Madagascar in 1669, traveling to the nearby island of Réunion. The relationship between the Malagasy and the remaining French continued to decline. Finally, in 1674, many of the French settlers were killed in a massacre. The survivors fled the island.

The Betsimisaraka people were the most diverse group on Madagascar. This photo was taken at the beginning of the 20th century.

No Man is an Island

While the Europeans were trying to figure out how to claim Madagascar, the Malagasy people were dividing into very different groups. Each of these kingdoms developed in a different region of the island. Among these groups were the Betsimisaraka, who established their kingdom in the east. The Menabe occupied the west, and the Merina ruled the interior highlands. The three groups developed independently of each other, largely because geography kept them separate from one another.

Of the three groups, the Betsimisaraka was the most racially diverse. Europeans, including pirates, visited the east coast of Madagascar often. Nosy Boraha, just off the east coast, quickly became an unofficial pirates' headquarters. A forty-gun fort was even erected there to protect their loot. Ratsimilaho, the son of a British pirate and a Malagasy woman, married a Malagasy princess from this region. He is said to have united the people of this Malagasy kingdom. The name Betsimisaraka means "those who stand together." When the European and American pirates were stopped by the British, the Betsimisaraka people took over the pirate trade. Living on this dangerous coast, they were already skilled sailors who were familiar with the trade winds. They seemed almost destined for the pirate trade.

The Merina kingdom had different goals. Its leader, Andrianampoinimerina, wanted to rule all the Malagasy. During his reign, from 1787 to 1810, he indeed expanded his territory significantly. Andrianampoinimerina also guided Madagascar in some positive directions.

Andrianampoinimerina

For example, he had a long-term plan for growing rice. He granted land to each family for rice farming, and focused on building canals to help with irrigation.

Andrianampoinimerina's son, King Radama I, ruled from 1810 to 1828. He continued the work his father had begun by expanding the Merina kingdom even further. The British formed an alliance with Radama I, which supplied him with weapons. He used the weapons to continue conquering the people of the island. If the people of the east coast had ever had any chance of defeating the Merina kingdom, it was now gone. Radama I now had an army of more than 35,000 well-armed soldiers.[1]

Even with this modern army, the Merina could not seem to conquer the Menabe kingdom. The Menabe king gave his daughter to be one of Radama I's wives, seeking peace. Radama I also continued to form relationships with the Europeans by including them in his government. He made an Englishman his advisor and a Frenchman the general of his army. Madagascar was becoming part of the modern world.

Radama I was making other types of changes to his young country as well. He welcomed British teachers to the island. The Protestant London Missionary Society opened schools and churches. Not only did many Malagasy learn how to read and write, but nearly a half-million of them also decided to become Protestant. Some students were even sent to Britain for further study.

Queen Ranavalona I, one of the wives of Radama I, allowed much less British influence during her reign from 1828 to 1861. In 1835, she outlawed Christianity altogether, killing many converts. These were difficult years for Malagasy who wanted religious freedom. Ranavalona I's son, Radama II took over the throne in 1861. His religious views seemed more in line with Radama I's. Sadly, Radama II was assassi-

Queen Ranavalona I

nated less than two years later, but not before he paved the way for religious freedom in Madagascar. By 1869, Christianity was the official religion of the Merina kingdom.

Madagascar was taking one step forward and two giant steps back. They had gained religious freedom, but they were beginning to lose control of their government. France began attacking Madagascar's ports in 1883. By 1890, the French had forced Britain out of the matter by way of a treaty that granted them sovereignty over Zanzibar. In 1896, France officially claimed Madagascar as a French colony.

The Merina monarchy was no more. France sent a governor-general named Joseph Simon Gallieni to Madagascar and exiled the Merina queen. Gallieni banned the use of English and made French the official language of this new Madagascar He even tried to suppress the Malagasy language that had been spoken on the island for centuries.

The Malagasy people were very unhappy with the direction in which their country was now heading. The colonists cleared forestland to grow coffee, cotton, and sugarcane. Malagasy people who couldn't afford to pay France's high taxes were forced to work on these plantations. They were treated like slaves. France expected much in return for this dreadful treatment. When World War I began in 1914, France demanded that the Malagasy join their fight. Understandably, the Malagasy resisted. They were tired of being dominated and wanted their freedom.

A resistance group of educated Malagasy banned together and formed the Vy Vato Sakelika (VVS). This group began as a secret society, and many members were jailed by the French when it was discovered. Still, the members didn't stop trying to bring change. The people wanted freedom and equal rights for everyone who lived on Madagascar. It wasn't until the end of World War II that France began allowing the Malagasy to have some say in their government. In 1946, Madagascar became an overseas territory, instead of a colony. This change enabled the island to send representatives to Paris and create a local government. Still, the political challenges weren't over. The Malagasy finally had some say, but they found it difficult to live and work with the French colonists. Just a year later, violent protests broke out on the island. As many as 80,000 Malagasy died.[2]

Change finally came when a man named Charles de Gaulle was elected president of France in 1958. Among the first things de Gaulle did in his new role was grant all French colonies their independence. For Madagascar, this defining moment occurred on June 26, 1960. The country was now a republic with its own elected president. His name was Philibert Tsiranana.

Philibert Tsiranana served as president of Madagascar from 1959 to 1972.

When Marc Ravalomanana claimed victory in the 2001 presidential election, Didier Ratsiraka responded by declaring martial law. He even moved the capital city from Antananarivo to Toamasina. For a short time, Madagascar had two presidents and two capitals.

Tsiranana wasn't the freethinking leader that the Malagasy had hoped he would be. He made numerous agreements with France when he finalized Madagascar's independence. The Malagasy felt like second-class citizens in what was now their own country. Their schools taught French culture and history. They wanted their children to learn Malagasy culture and history—from Malagasy teachers. When 100,000 students went on strike over the matter, the government closed the schools in response.[3]

The educational system wasn't the only problem under Tsiranana. The country was in a state of constant turmoil. There were economic troubles, ethnic tension, and even suspicion of corruption. It seemed that Tsiranana had put many of his friends in positions of power when he took the presidency. He eventually realized that his actions—and in some cases, his inaction—weren't going to be tolerated by the Malagasy. He dissolved the government on May 18, 1972, then resigned his position.

Madagascar's Second Republic began three years later. Upon Tsiranana's resignation, the army appointed Lieutenant Commander Didier Ratsiraka as the new head of state. On December 21, 1975, he was officially elected president. Ratsiraka was a socialist who greatly admired the political system of North Korea. He wanted total control over every part of the country, especially its economy. He virtually closed Madagascar to foreigners, especially those from the West. This move only worsened the country's economy.

Ratsiraka ruled Madagascar for the next seventeen years. When it became apparent that the people wanted to remove him from the presidency, he did everything he could to hold on to his powerful position. He even tried to rig the voting process. In the end, his efforts were unsuccessful. The people made it clear that they wanted him out of office.

Albert Zafy

On March 27, 1993, Madagascar's Third Republic was formed. The country had yet another new constitution and another new president. Albert Zafy became the third leader of this still-young nation. Zafy had trouble getting along with many people both inside and outside the government. He was facing the near-impossible task of solving Madagascar's many economic problems, and he couldn't solve them on his own. The International Monetary Fund (IMF) and the World Bank were willing to help, but they demanded many big changes in exchange. Zafy feared that these changes were too risky. He was impeached a little more than three years after he was elected.

In a surprising turn of events, the people of Madagascar then re-elected Didier Ratsiraka as president. Other candidates ran against him, but Ratsiraka was familiar. He also seemed to understand that his old ways of ruling the country weren't going to work this time. He agreed to open the country for trade and other important types of economic development. After he was elected, his unwillingness to accept the people's wishes continued, however.

When he lost his bid for reelection to Marc Ravalomanana in 2001, Ratsiraka refused to acknowledge the outcome. After a high court ruled that Ravalomanana had indeed won the election, Ratsiraka fled to

Marc
Ravalomanana

France. Ravalomanana remained in office for several years, but in March of 2009 a man who led protests against Ravalomanana became the country's new leader. Andry Rajoelina began his political career as the mayor of Antananarivo, an area in the central part of the island where he was born. A successful businessman, Rajoelina was just thirty-four years old when he took office as president. Because Rajoclina was not elected, he has promised to hold fair elections in the near future. After being postponed multiple times, presidential elections are currently planned for May 8, 2013. A second round of elections will take place on July 3, 2013. No one knows for certain if the elections will be delayed yet again.

For all the conflict, however, there has also been some progress on this island nation. In 2005, Moana Essa Raseta became the first female governor of Ihorombe, a region in southeastern Madagascar. When Raseta was born in 1960, it was unheard of for a woman to perform such a duty. Today, however, she helps other females gain access to education. "Women and girls should study," she says. "It is their right, and, more importantly, they rely too much on men here. They should be able to rely on themselves."[4]

The government of Madagascar faces many challenges, like what to do about the destruction caused by tavy. The process can transform a primary forest into land that is unusable, like this area in Isalo National Park.

Chapter 5

Playing Its Part in the World

Today, Madagascar's governmental structure is similar to that of many other republics of the world. It consists of an executive branch, a legislative branch, and a judicial branch. The executive branch is made up of the president, the prime minister, and their cabinet. The president is elected by citizens 18 years of age or older. This person then works with the country's prime minister, who is appointed by the president. The prime minister consequently appoints thirty people to make up the cabinet, which is called The Council of Ministers. Each cabinet department is responsible for a different aspect of the government. For example, the minister of agriculture oversees farming.

The people elect a president to one five-year term. If the president chooses to run for reelection and wins, an additional five-year term follows. A certain amount of tension remains between the Merina and côtiers, the people who live on the coast. In 1992, the new constitution dictated that when the president is from the highlands, the prime minister is selected from the coastal region. Conversely, if the president is a Merina, the prime minster is chosen from the côtiers. Nevertheless, in 2007 both the president (Marc Ravalomanana) and the prime minister (Charles Rabemananjara) were Merinas.

The legislative branch is called parliament. It consists of the National Assembly and the Senate. The National Assembly is much like our House of Representatives in the United States. National Assembly members are elected by the people. The exact number each region has depends on its population. Each member serves a term of four years.

The Senate in Madagascar, however, is set up much differently than the U.S. Senate. One-third of the members of Madagascar's Senate are chosen by the president. The rest are selected by an Electoral College.

The judicial branch is made up of an eleven-member Supreme Court and a nine-member High Constitutional Court. The Supreme Court is the highest court that rules on matters that concern the people. The High Constitutional Court hears cases involving governmental changes.

Madagascar is now divided into six provinces, which are similar to states. Antsiranana lies in the north of the country. Toamasina is in the northeast, with Mahajanga in the northwest. Antananarivo is located in the center. Toliara is found in the southwest, with Fianarantsoa in the southeast.

Farming remains a vital part of Malagasy culture. Many families still use a part of their land to grow their own rice. Farming has also become an important part of Madagascar's economy. The most common cash crops are coffee, cloves, sisal, sugarcane, and vanilla. Agricultural products like these make up more than a quarter of the country's exports.[1]

A Malagasy girl pollinating vanilla flowers

When a conflict or dispute comes up between Malagasy community members, elders hold meetings to discuss and solve small issues within the village. They call this system *fokonolona*.

Tavy continues to be a source of great controversy in Madagascar. Because this practice destroys the land for up to twenty years, the government has declared tavy illegal. Still, many Malagasy risk imprisonment by using this slash-and-burn farming method anyway. Tavy helps the farmers grow rice much faster in the short-term, but it creates an ongoing long-term problem that could have a dreadful effect on the country's future.

Another popular export is fish. Being a country surrounded by water, Madagascar is home to many varieties of fish and other seafood. Shrimp in particular thrive on farms in the swamplands of the country. Fish production has increased significantly over the last few decades. The value of Madagascar's seafood exports has topped $100 million U.S.[2]

The Malagasy welcome tourists to fish in their waters as well. Although the number of visitors to the island is relatively small, fishing enthusiasts can charter boats off the northwest coast. This area is extremely rich in sailfish, giant trevally, dorado, king mackerel, barracuda, wahoo, and dog tooth tuna.

A sailfish takes hold of a fishing lure

Numerous bird species inhabit the island. The Malagasy Pond Heron is an endangered member of the Ardeidae family, which includes over sixty species of herons worldwide.

Chapter 6

A Different Kind of Vacation

Tourism is still a new business for Madagascar. Although the island has much to offer its visitors, it hasn't been as successful in attracting them as neighboring islands like Mauritius and the Seychelles have been. Madagascar has only a small number of hotels. Its roads and transportation services are also less dependable than those of more popular vacation spots. Visitors who don't mind roughing it a little can still have a great time on the island. The country is unlikely to create a large tourism base, however, until it improves its hospitality industry.

There are a few conventional tourist attractions in Madagascar. These include the Tsimbazaza, a museum with botanical gardens and a zoo in the capital city of Antananarivo. Travelers can also visit the Rova, a royal palace in the highlands. Another popular attraction is the Royal Hill of Ambohimanga, also in the highlands.

The best attractions by far on Madagascar are the natural ones. Tourists can visit several nature reserves on the island. Périnet is just east of Antananarivo. Berenty and Kaleta Park are both in the southern region of the island. Visitors to these protected areas can hike along the trails and see the plants and wildlife that most others only get to read about in books. One can easily spend an entire day at each reserve. Although the reserves don't bring large amounts of money into Madagascar's economy, they do create jobs for the Malagasy. Each reserve needs guides, wardens, and other staff members to keep it running.

The Spiny Desert is the perfect place to see numerous types of interesting plants and animals. About 95 percent of the plants you can see there are found nowhere else on earth.[1] (And yes, as the name implies, most are covered with sharp spines.) Desert animals include the Grandidier's mongoose, the radiated tortoise of Madagascar, and the ring-tailed lemur.

More than half of the people who visit Madagascar today are French. Another 10 percent of the visitors come from the nearby island of Réunion.[2] Currently, very few Americans travel to Madagascar. However, many Americans are there as part of the Peace Corps, an organization of volunteers who travel to needy foreign lands. While there, volunteers provide the people with basic medical care and education. For example, they may teach children to read and write, or provide parents with instructions for good nutrition.

A group of Peace Corps volunteers in Madagascar sings traditional Malagasy songs.

A market in Antananarivo

If you ever visit Madagascar, be sure to check out the local crafts. Open-air markets are plentiful in Antananarivo, with all sorts of handmade items. The Malagasy produce beautiful baskets, mats and rugs, and wood carvings. Malagasy woodworkers from Ambositra use a special technique called marquetry to make magnificent inlaid wooden boxes. They are made of colored woods that fit together like puzzle pieces. The Malagasy are also incredibly talented with needles and embroidery thread. The wives of British missionaries brought this craft to the island, but the Malagasy have put their own spin on it. They create amazing scenes on all sorts of fabrics using their everyday lives as inspiration.

FYI FACT:

The open-air markets in Madagascar have no set prices. If you see something you like, make an offer. Be prepared to do some bartering, but you are sure to find some wonderful bargains.

A group of children hold up a flag in celebration of a famadihana. Also called a bone-turning ceremony, this ritual commemorates the life of a loved one who has died.

Culture and Lifestyle

The Malagasy culture is deeply rooted in their traditional religious beliefs. Even the people who have converted to Christianity still respect many of the tenets of their ancestors' theology. It is especially important to the Malagasy to honor their dead. They believe that distant relatives still play roles in the people's everyday lives. They look to these family members for guidance, and they fear that bad things will happen if they do not pay proper tribute to them.

Even after a relative has been dead a long time, the Malagasy continue to include them in their lives through special ceremonies. One of these is a bone-turning ceremony called *famadihana*. Family members gather together to celebrate the life of this person—and to share stories about things that have happened in the family since the person died. During the ceremony, the remains of this person are dug up so they can be passed around. Families perform this ritual every five to seven years, or as often as they can afford to do so. A famadihana can be expensive. The whole village participates, and numerous foods are prepared for the celebration.

The dead remain a large part of the Malagasy culture in more ways than one. The people construct ornate tombs for burial. Malagasy invest large amounts of time, effort, and money into creating these structures. Many tombs are nicer than the people's homes. Bodies are wrapped in silk shrouds, which are replaced each time a bone-turning ceremony is performed.

Another part of daily life in Madagascar is called *fady*. This word refers to the people's beliefs about things they should and shouldn't do. Americans might call fady manners. Fady also refers to off-limits actions, things we would call taboo. For example, the Malagasy do not eat pork. They would therefore call this type of meat fady. Other types of fady are more superstitious in nature. People from different areas of Madagascar believe that different days of the week are the most or least suitable for doing certain types of things. Holding a Merina funeral on a Tuesday is said to cause a second death, for instance.

Music is also a big part of life on the island. The Malagasy not only have their own type of music, but they also have their own unique instruments to play it. These include the *kabosy,* the *marovany,* and the *valiha.* The kabosy is an instrument that looks like a box-shaped guitar. The marovany is a stringed instrument with a metal or wooden sound box. The valiha is a bamboo tube with between twelve and twenty-two attached strings.

A man plays Malagasy music on a kabosy, a instrument that looks like a small, boxed-shaped guitar.

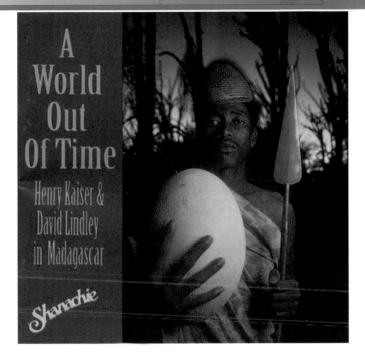

A World Out of Time **album cover**

The complex rhythms of Malagasy music often sound odd to people from other areas when they first hear them. As people have discovered Malagasy music, though, it has become more popular in the West. Some westerners even play this music on their own guitars. In 1991, two American guitarists named Henry Kaiser and David Lindley helped to introduce Malagasy music to the rest of the world when they traveled to Madagascar to record an album. Playing the music on their guitars, they were accompanied by numerous Malagasy musicians and their traditional instruments. The second volume of their album, *A World Out of Time,* was even nominated for a Grammy Award.[1]

One of the best-known musicians from Madagascar is Paul Bert Rahasimanana. He goes by the nickname Rossy. When Rossy began

FYI FACT:

In Madagascar, gray geese are thought to be bad luck, but gray-haired people may keep them. The human's gray hair is said to cancel out the fady of the gray geese.

Paul Bert
Rahasimanana

performing, he didn't even use instruments. Instead, he followed the beat of hand-clapping. When he added music into the mix, he became even more popular. Soon he was performing concerts and playing his songs on the radio. He even toured overseas in the 1980s. His most famous album is called *Island of Ghosts*. This title is fitting in light of the role the dead play in Malagasy culture. Rossy also sings about hope, love, and poverty.

Another popular Malagasy musician is Dama Mahaleo. He is especially beloved in Madagascar, where he is known as the country's musical poet. You can hear both Rossy's and Mahaleo's music played on Kaiser and Lindley's *A World Out of Time* series, which now includes three volumes.

Many authors have come from Madagascar as well, including Michèle Rakotoson, the daughter of a journalist and a librarian. Born in Antananarivo in 1948, Rakotoson published her first novel in 1984.

Entitled *Dadabé,* the book was inspired by her childhood experiences vacationing with her grandfather in the countryside. In addition to several novels, Rakotoson has written plays and short stories. She has lived in France and the United States, but currently resides in Madagascar, where she is active in politics.

Under the law, Malagasy children are required to attend school from the age of six to fourteen.[2] Still, more than 400,000 kids six to ten do not attend.[3] Although enrollment is free, many families have a hard time paying for necessary supplies such as pencils, workbooks, and uniforms. Limited education and limited job opportunities make the future an uncertain one for many young Malagasy.

Malagasy students

Hira Gasy is a weekly Malagasy tradition that is held in Antananarivo. The celebration combines speeches and music.

Chapter 8

Celebrations in Madagascar

Whether you enjoy music and dancing, or crafts and storytelling, you are sure to find something fun to do during a stay in Madagascar. Festivals take place throughout the year. Many of them occur in the fall and winter—Madagascar's fall and winter that is.

Alahamady Be is a two-day festival that celebrates Madagascar's New Year. It takes place when the first new moon in the first month of the year appears in March. The Malagasy gather to eat, sing, and exchange gifts during this time. Just like Americans gather in New York City to watch its famous ball drop, the Malagasy have a special place where many of them celebrate the beginning of their new year. They put on their best and brightest clothing and head to the Royal Hill of Ambohimanga. They listen to music and pray to their ancestors who made the trip before them to this sacred spot.

Following the prayers, it is time to eat. Families celebrating Alahadamy Be dine on smoked sausages, vegetables, and *zebu* (cattle) meat. Adults drink wine made from cane sugar or rice. Perhaps the most important dish at this event is *romazava*, the national dish of Madagascar.[1] It is made with flavorful herbs and leaves. Like many Malagasy dishes, romazava is served with *vary* (rice).

Public speaking is another important part of Malagasy culture. On Sundays, speeches are combined with music for a tradition called *Hira Gasy*. Also performed on special occasions, Hira Gasy takes place in Antananarivo. Elders who are skilled speech-makers begin by giving their advice to the younger generations. Hira Gasy is anything but a

Even the youngest members of Malagasy culture take part in Alahamady Be.

boring lecture, however. The elders also tell jokes and fables to make it as entertaining as possible. The themes are usually simple, focusing on the importance of family and following Malagasy traditions.

The speech is followed by an exciting musical performance. Two teams, consisting of both men and women, compete in front of the crowd. They dress in 19th-century-style attire. The women wear long, brightly colored matching gowns. The men wear red jackets and straw hats. Both wear shawls called *lambas.* The band plays music on drums, violins, and wind instruments. Performances can last for the bulk of the day, with the crowd picking the winner at the end.[2]

Because so many Malagasy are Catholic, another popular holiday in Madagascar is All Saints' Day. On the first day of November each year, the Malagasy gather to honor people who have lived devoted religious lives. Families begin the day by dressing in their best clothes

All Saints' Day parade

and going to church at dawn. Children place candles on the church's altar. They then place garlands made of special foods on the statues of saints as offerings.

The parishioners gather outside the church to form a parade. The procession is led by a person carrying a statue of the Virgin Mary. At the end of the parade, everyone returns to the church and prays together once more. When the services are over, the feast begins. Although the holiday is a serious one, the mood is not at all sad. A strong, positive connection with the dead is part of all Malagasy culture.

FYI FACT:

Many other countries celebrate All Saints' Day, too. The French, who brought this holiday to Madagascar, call it *La Toussaint.*

Banana Fritters

Always have an adult supervise when working in the kitchen

Ingredients:
6   well-ripened bananas
1   cup flour
¼ cup sugar
¼ cup milk
1   teaspoon nutmeg
1   teaspoon vanilla
2   tablespoons oil

Directions:
1. Mash bananas with a fork, potato masher, or food processor.
2. Add flour and mix.
3. Mix milk, vanilla, and sugar together. Add these wet ingredients to banana mixture along with the nutmeg. The batter should resemble pancake batter. You may need to add a little more milk at this time. Mix well.
4. Spoon batter into small pancake-sized circles in a nonstick frying pan or on a griddle, coated with oil, for about 2 minutes on each side over medium heat. The finished fritters should be a warm, golden brown.

Raffia Placemats

Raffia is a fiber that comes from Madagascar's raffia palm trees. The Malagasy use raffia to create baskets, hats, handbags, and more. Many of these items can be found in Madagascar's open-air markets.

Supplies:
Raffia (in at least two different colors)
Poster board
Yard stick
Pencil
Scissors
Tape

Directions:
1. Cut the poster board into four rectangles or squares of equal area, about the size of a table setting.
2. Tape one end of raffia to one corner of the poster board. This will be the placemat's base color. Then, wind it around the poster board (either vertically or horizontally) over and over until you have covered the entire area.
3. Weave your other raffia colors through the placemat, going in the opposite direction—over one strand, under the next, over the next, and so on. You may choose to make a simple or elaborate pattern. You might also choose to make all four placemats the same, or entirely different from one another.
4. When you are done with each raffia strand, tuck it into a corner on the bottom of the placemat and tape it.

ca. 300 B.C.E.	Indonesians settle on the island of Madagascar.
600s C.E.	Arab traders arrive, bringing Islam to Madagascar.
ca. 1300	Explorer Marco Polo is the first to use the name Madagascar, although he never actually visits the island.
1500	Diego Dias becomes the first European to explore Madagascar, calling it São Lourenço.
1600s-1700s	British traders and colonists arrive.
1648	Étienne de Flacourt takes over a French settlement on Madagascar.
1669	French settlers leave Madagascar.
1710	Betsimisaraka leader Ratsimilaho defeats king Ramanano, extending his rule.
1787	Andrianampoinimerina becomes leader of the Merina people.
1810	Radama I becomes the new ruler of the Merina kingdom.
1820	The first mission school opens on Madagascar.
1828	Queen Ranavalona I becomes the new ruler of the Merina people, later eliminating European influence in Madagascar.
1835	Christianity is outlawed in the Merina kingdom by Queen Ranavalona I.
1861	King Radama II takes over. He encourages British and French traders and missionaries to return to the island, and allows religious freedom in Madagascar.
1863	Radama II is assassinated.
1869	Merina kingdom makes Christianity its official religion.
1885	Madagascar becomes a French protectorate.
1896	Madagascar becomes a French colony.
1913	Vy Vato Sakelika, a secret society seeking Malagasy freedom, is formed.
1946	Madagascar becomes a French territory.
1947	Malagasy people begin revolt against France, resulting in 80,000 or more Malagasy deaths.
1958	Madagascar becomes a self-governing French state.
1959	Philibert Tsiranana is elected president.
1960	Madagascar officially becomes the Malagasy Republic, an independent nation.
1972	Tsiranana dissolves the government and resigns his position.
1975	Didier Ratsiraka officially elected president; Malagasy Republic becomes Madagascar.
1993	Albert Zafy is elected president; Madagascar's Third Republic is formed.
1996	Zafy is impeached.
1997	Ratsiraka is reelected president.
2001	Marc Ravalomanana elected president; Ratsiraka refuses to step down and attempts to create new capital city.
2009	Andry Rajoelina takes over as interim president.
2011	Omer Beriziky is announced as new prime minister, in an attempt to help transition the government.
2012	Presidential elections originally scheduled for this year are postponed until 2013.

CHAPTER NOTES

Chapter 1. Much More Than a Movie
1. The World Bank Group, "World Development Report 2003," Sustainable Development in a Dynamic Economy, http://www.dynamicsustainabledevelopment.org/showsection.php?file=chapter8c2.htm
2. NASA Earth Observatory, "Betsiboka Estuary, Madagascar," http://eol.jsc.nasa.gov/EarthObservatory/BetsibokaEstuaryMadagascar.htm
3. Mark Eveleigh, *Travel Intelligence,* "Madagascar—the Island Continent," http://www.travelintelligence.com/travel-writing/madagascar-%E2%80%93-island-continent

Chapter 2. So Close, Yet So Far
1. BBC, "Madagascar Floods Worse Than Thought," March 15, 2000, http://news.bbc.co.uk/2/hi/africa/678808.stm
2. Encyclopedia of the Nations, "Madagascar," http://www.nationsencyclopedia.com/geography/Indonesia-to-Mongolia/Madagascar.html
3. Ibid.
4. Joy Schochet, *Rainforest Primer,* "Biodiversity: Plants," Rainforest Conservation Fund, http://www.rainforestconservation.org/rainforest-primer/2-biodiversity/e-plants
5. Royal Botanic Gardens, "Orchid Conservation in Madagascar," http://www.kew.org/plants/orchids/madagascar.html
6. Hilary Bradt, *Madagascar* (Bucks, England: Bradt Travel Guides, 2011), p. 57.

Chapter 3. A Short History, A Long Struggle
1. D.A. Burney, et al., *Journal of Human Evolution,* "A chronology for late prehistoric Madagascar," vol. 47, July-August 2004, pp. 25-63.
2. Wild Madagascar, "People," http://www.wildmadagascar.org/people/
3. Adrian Room, *Placenames of the World* (Jefferson, NC: McFarland & Company, 2006), p. 230.

Chapter 4. No Man is an Island
1. Helen Chapin Metz, "Madagascar: A Country Study," Washington, D.C.: Library of Congress, 1995.
2. Sidney Lens and Howard Zinn, *The Forging of the American Empire* (London, England: Pluto Press, 2003), p. 331.
3. Helen Chapin Metz, "Madagascar: A Country Study," Washington, D.C.: Library of Congress, 1995.
4. Unicef, "Using Political Clout to Empower Women in Madagascar," December 10, 2006, http://www.unicef.org/infobycountry/madagascar_37440.html

Chapter 5. Playing Its Part in the World
1. The World Bank, "Madagascar," 2012, http://data.worldbank.org/country/madagascar

2. Alexander Simoes, "Trade in Madagascar," The Observatory of Economic Complexity, http://atlas.media.mit.edu/country/mdg/

Chapter 6. A Different Kind of Vacation
1. Christopher McLeod, "Androy Forests," Sacred Land Film Project, http://www.sacredland.org/androy-forests/
2. Economic Development Board of Madagascar, "The island of megadiversity," http://www.edbm.gov.mg/page-tourism-4-3

Chapter 7. Culture and Lifestyle
1. Variety Staff, "Grammy Nominees," *Variety,* http://www.variety.com/article/VR117230?refCatId=16
2. Helen Chapin Metz, "Madagascar: A Country Study," Washington, D.C.: Library of Congress, 1995.
3. Unicef, "Madagascar," http://www.unicef.org/madagascar/5514_6478.html

Chapter 8. Celebrations in Madagascar
1. Private Safaris, "Madagascar Travel Tips," http://www.privatesafaris.com/madagascar-travel.html
2. Zambezi Safari & Travel Company, "Antananarivo," http://www.zambezi.com/location/antananarivo

FURTHER READING

Books
Bishop, Nic. *Digging for Bird-Dinosaurs: An Expedition to Madagascar.* New York: Houghton Mifflin, 2000.
Kabana, Joni. *Torina's World—A Child's Life in Madagascar.* Portland, Oregon: Arnica Publishing, 2007.
Manser, Riaan. *Around Madagascar on my Kayak.* Jeppestown, South Africa: Jonathan Ball Publishing, 2011.
Throp, Claire. *Lemurs.* Portsmouth, NH: Heineman-Raintree, 2012.

On the Internet
National Geographic, "Madagascar"
    http://travel.nationalgeographic.com/travel/countries/madagascar-guide/
Peace Corps, "Madagascar"
    http://www.peacecorps.gov/index.cfm?shell=learn.wherepc.africa&cntry=madagascar
St. Louis Zoo, Center for Conservation in Madagascar
    http://www.stlzoo.org/conservation/wildcare-institute/lemursinmadagascar/
Wild Madagascar
    http://www.wildmadagascar.org/kids/

Bradt, Hilary. *Madagascar.* Bucks, England: Bradt Travel Guides, 2011.

Burney, D.A., et al. "A chronology for late prehistoric Madagascar." *Journal of Human Evolution,* July-August 2004.

Cougar Mountain Zoo: "World of Lemurs," http://www.cougarmountainzoo.org/The%20 Animals/ringtailedlemurfact.aspx

Economic Development Board of Madagascar: "The island of megadiversity," http://www. edbm.gov.mg/page-tourism-4-3

Encyclopedia of the Nations: "Madagascar," http://www.nationsencyclopedia.com/ geography/Indonesia-to-Mongolia/Madagascar.html

Eveleigh, Mark. "Madagascar—the Island Continent." *Travel Intelligence.* http://www. travelintelligence.com/travel-writing/madagascar-%E2%80%93-island-continent

Garbutt, Nick. *Mammals of Madagascar.* New Haven, Connecticut: Yale University Press, 2007.

Jolly, Alison. *Lords and Lemurs.* Boston, Massachusetts: Houghton, Mifflin, Harcourt, 2004.

Lens, Sidney, and Howard Zinn. *The Forging of the American Empire.* London, England: Pluto Press, 2003.

"Madagascar Floods Worse Than Thought." BBC, March 15, 2000. http://news.bbc.co.uk/2/ hi/africa/678808.stm

"Madagascar." The World Bank, 2012. http://data.worldbank.org/country/madagascar

McLeod, Christopher. "Androy Forests." Sacred Land Film Project. http://www.sacredland. org/androy-forests/

Metz, Helen Chapin. "Madagascar: A Country Study." Washington, D.C.: Library of Congress, 1995.

NASA Earth Observatory: "Betsiboka Estuary, Madagascar," http://eol.jsc.nasa.gov/ EarthObservatory/BetsibokaEstuaryMadagascar.htm

Private Safaris: "Madagascar Travel Tips," http://www.privatesafaris.com/madagascar-travel. html

Randrianja, Solofo, and Stephen Ellis. *Madagascar: A Short History.* Chicago, Illinois: University of Chicago Press, 2009.

Room, Adrian. *Placenames of the World.* Jefferson, NC: McFarland & Company, 2006.

Royal Botanic Gardens: "Orchid Conservation in Madagascar," http://www.kcw.org/plants/ orchids/madagascar.html

Schochet, Joy. "Biodiversity: Plants." *Rainforest Primer,* Rainforest Conservation Fund. http:// www.rainforestconservation.org/rainforest-primer/2-biodiversity/e-plants

Simoes, Alexander. "Trade in Madagascar." The Observatory of Economic Complexity. http://atlas.media.mit.edu/country/mdg/

Unicef: "Madagascar," http://www.unicef.org/madagascar/5514_6478.html

Unicef: "Using Political Clout to Empower Women in Madagascar." December 10, 2006. http://www.unicef.org/infobycountry/madagascar_37440.html

U.S. Department of State, Bureau of African Affairs: "Madagascar," http://www.state.gov/r/ pa/ei/bgn/5460.htm

Variety Staff, "Grammy Nominees," *Variety,* http://www.variety.com/article/ VR117230?refCatId=16

Volet, Jean-Marie. "Michèle Rakotoson." *Reading Women Writers and African Literatures.* The University of Western Australia, September 22, 2010. http://aflit.arts.uwa.edu.au/ RakotosonMicheleEng.html

Wild Madagascar: "People," http://www.wildmadagascar.org/people/

The World Bank Group: "World Development Report 2003." Sustainable Development in a Dynamic Economy. http://www.dynamicsustainabledevelopment.org/showsection. php?file=chapter8c2.htm

Zambezi Safari & Travel Company, "Antananarivo," http://www.zambezi.com/location/ antananarivo

GLOSSARY

barter (BAHR-ter): to trade by exchanging items rather than money

cabinet (KAB-uh-nit): council advising a president

charter (CHAHR-ter): to hire for exclusive use

colonize (KOL-uh-nahyz): to establish a settlement in a new land

conservation (KON-ser-vey-shuhn): the official supervision of an area of land to prevent its loss or damage

convert (kon-VERT): to persuade a person to change from one religion to another

dormant (DAWR-muhnt): in a state of rest or inactivity

economy (ih-KON-uh-mee): the management of resources of a community

garland (GAHR-luhnd): a wreath of flowers, leaves, or other material

hospitality (hos-pi-TAL-i-tee): the friendly reception of guests or strangers

impeach (im-PEECH): to accuse of misconduct in office

migrate (MAHY-greyt): to move from one region to another

navigate (NAV-i-geyt): to direct a ship on its course

politics (POL-i-tiks): the science or art of government

precipitation (prih-sip-i-TEY-shuhn): the falling of rain, snow, or hail

shroud (SHROUD): a cloth in which a corpse is wrapped for burial

topsoil (TOP-soil): the fertile, upper part of the soil

agriculture   10, 12, 13, 16, 32, 33, 38, 39, 40-41
Alahamady Be   53, 54
Andrianampoinimerina   31-32
Antananarivo   13, 16, 35, 37, 40, 43, 45, 50, 52, 53
Antsiranana   40
arts   45, 48-54
baobab tree   13, 20-21, 26
Berenty Reserve   23, 43
Betsiboka River   13, 18
Betsimisaraka   30-31
Britain   29, 31, 32, 33, 45
celebrations   52-55
Central High Plateau   16
chameleon   24-25
Christianity   13, 29, 32-33, 47, 54-55
climate   7, 10, 13, 17-18
coral reef   18-19
côtiers   39
cuisine   53
culture   46-55
de Flacourt, Étienne   29
de Gaulle, Charles   34
Dias, Diego   28-29
economy   13, 35, 36, 40-41, 43
education   32, 35, 37, 44, 51
English (language)   13, 33
fady   47-48, 49
famadihana   46, 47
Fianarantsoa   40
fossa   24, 25
France   29, 32, 33-35, 37, 44, 51, 55
French (language)   13, 33
Gallieni, Joseph Simon   33
geography   7, 9-10, 12, 14, 15-19
government   34-37, 38, 39-40, 41, 51
health   17, 21, 29, 44
Hira Gasy   52, 53-54
history   27-37
Homo sapiens   6
Indian Ocean   7, 9, 17, 27
Indonesia   27
Isalo National Park   38
Islam   13, 27, 29
Kaiser, Henry   49, 50
Kaleta Park   43
language   13, 28, 29, 33
lemur   8, 9-10, 14, 19, 21-24, 44
Lindley, David   49, 50
Mahajanga   40
Mahaleo, Dama   50
Malagasy (language)   12, 13, 28, 29, 33
marine life   17, 18-19, 41
Maroantsetra   17

Maromokotro   13, 16
Menabe   31, 32
Merina   31-33, 39, 48
Mozambique Channel   7, 9, 15, 25
music   48-50, 52, 53-54
Nosy Be   14, 15
Nosy Boraha (Saint-Marie)   15, 31
Nosy Komba   14
orchid   19-20
Pangaea   9
parks   12, 23, 38, 43
Peace Corps   44
Périnet   43
pirates   31
Polo, Marco   28
Portugal   28, 29
provinces   40
Rabemananjara, Charles   39
Radama I   32
Radama II   32-33
Rahasimanana, Paul Bert (Rossy)   49-50
Rajoelina, Andry   37
Rakotoson, Michèle   50-51
Ranavalona I   32, 33
Raseta, Moana Essa   37
Ratsimilaho   31
Ratsiraka, Didier   35, 36
Ravalomanana, Marc   35, 36-37, 39
ravinala palm tree   20
religion   13, 27, 29, 32-33, 46, 47, 53, 54-55
Réunion   29, 44
rivers   13, 17, 18, 19
Rova   43
Royal Hill of Ambohimanga   43, 53
Somalia   28
Spiny Desert   44
sports   13
tavy   10, 12, 38, 41
Toamasina   13, 35, 40
Toliara   19, 40
tourism   22-23, 41, 43-45, 53
trade   27-28, 35, 36
Tsiranana, Philibert   34-35
United States   17, 31, 39-40, 48, 49, 51, 53
Vazimba   27
vegetation   7, 9, 10, 12, 13, 17, 19-20, 26, 43-44
Vy Vato Sakelika (VVS)   33
wildlife   7, 8, 9-10, 14, 17, 18-19, 21-25, 42, 43-44, 49
World War I   33
World War II   34
Zafy, Albert   36

Tammy Gagne is the author of numerous books for both adults and children, including *The Nile River* and *We Visit South Africa* for Mitchell Lane Publishers. One of her favorite pastimes is visiting schools to speak to children about the writing process. She resides in northern New England with her husband, son, and a menagerie of animals.